GW00536998

The Dancers of Colbek

William Bedford is an award-winning poet, short-story writer, children's novelist and novelist, his work appearing in *Agenda, Critical Quarterly, Encounter, The Daily Telegraph, Essays in Criticism, The Independent Magazine, The International Literary Quarterly, The John Clare Society Journal, London Magazine, London Review of Books, The Nation (New York), The New Statesman, Poetry Review, The Southern Review, The Tablet, The Ted Hughes Society Journal, Temenos, The Warwick Review, The Washington Times* and many others around the world.

His novel *Happiland* was shortlisted for the 1990 *Guardian* Fiction Prize. His selected poems, *Collecting Bottle Tops*, and selected short stories, *None of the Cadillacs Was Pink*, were both published in 2009. His poem 'Then' won First Prize in the 2014 Roundel Poetry Competition. His poem 'The Journey' won First Prize in the 2014 *London Magazine* International Poetry Competition. A short story, 'The Herring Lass', was shortlisted for the 2014 *London Magazine* International Short Story Competition. Red Squirrel Press published *The Fen Dancing* in March 2014 and *The Bread Horse* in October 2015. Dempsey & Windle published *Chagall's Circus* in 2019.

Also by Two Rivers Poets

David Attwooll, *The Sound Ladder* (2015)
Kate Behrens, *The Beholder* (2012)
Kate Behrens, *Man with Bombe Alaska* (2016)
Kate Behrens, *Penumbra* (2019)
Adrian Blamires & Peter Robinson (eds.), *The Arts of Peace* (2014)
Conor Carville, *English Martyrs* (2019)
David Cooke, *A Murmuration* (2015)
Terry Cree, *Fruit* (2014)
Claire Dyer, *Eleven Rooms* (2013)
Claire Dyer, *Interference Effects* (2016)
John Froy, *Sandpaper & Seahorses* (2018)
A. F. Harrold, *The Point of Inconvenience* (2013)
Maria Teresa Horta, *Point of Honour* translated by Lesley Saunders (2019)
Ian House, *Nothing's Lost* (2014)
Gill Learner, *Chill Factor* (2016)
Sue Leigh, *Chosen Hill* (2018)
Becci Louise, *Octopus Medicine* (2017)
Mairi MacInnes, *Amazing Memories of Childhood, etc.* (2016)
Steven Matthews, *On Magnetism* (2017)
Henri Michaux, *Storms under the Skin* translated by Jane Draycott (2017)
James Peake, *Reaction Time of Glass* (2019)
Tom Phillips, *Recreation Ground* (2012)
John Pilling & Peter Robinson (eds.), *The Rilke of Ruth Speirs:*
    New Poems, Duino Elegies, Sonnets to Orpheus & Others (2015)
Peter Robinson, *Foreigners, Drunks and Babies: Eleven Stories* (2013)
Peter Robinson, *The Constitutionals: A Fiction* (2019)
Lesley Saunders, *Cloud Camera* (2012)
Lesley Saunders, *Nominy-Dominy* (2018)
Jack Thacker, *Handling* (2018)
Susan Utting, *Fair's Fair* (2012)
Susan Utting, *Half the Human Race* (2017)
Jean Watkins, *Scrimshaw* (2013)
Jean Watkins, *Precarious Lives* (2018)

The Dancers of Colbek

William Bedford

TWO
RIVERS
PRESS

First published in the UK in 2020 by Two Rivers Press
7 Denmark Road, Reading RG1 5PA.
www.tworiverspress.com

ISBN 978-1-909747-57-9

1 2 3 4 5 6 7 8 9

Two Rivers Press is represented in the UK by Inpress Ltd
and distributed by NBNi.

Cover design and illustrations by Sally Castle
Author photograph by Tim O'Leary
Text design by Nadja Guggi and typeset in Janson and Parisine

Printed and bound in Great Britain by Imprint Digital, Exeter

Acknowledgements

Acknowledgements are due to the editors of the following magazines in which versions of some these poems first appeared: *Acumen, Agenda, Allegro Poetry Magazine, The Cannon's Mouth, Confluence, Domestic Cherry, The Frogmore Papers, The High Window, Ink Sweat & Tears, The Interpreter's House, The International Literary Quarterly, John Clare Society Journal, London Grip, The London Magazine, The New Statesman, New Walk, Pennine Platform, Poetry Salzburg Review, The Poetry Shed* and *Temenos*.

Acknowledgements are also due to Professor Jonathan Bate for his *John Clare: A Biography*, and to Professor Simon Kövesi, for his *John Clare: Nature, Criticism and History*, and for his support and conversation.

Professor Norman Francis Blake guided me through my undergraduate studies of Middle English poetry and prose, and introduced me to Robert Mannyng of Brunne's *Handlyng Synne*, most especially the tale 'The Dancers of Colbek'.

'Then' won first prize in the 2014 Roundel Poetry Competition. It was included in the anthology *Something Happens, Sometimes Here*, Ed. Rory Waterman (Five Leaves Publications, 2015).

'The Journey' won first prize in the 2014 *London Magazine* International Poetry Competition. It was included in the anthology *Something Happens, Sometimes Here*, Ed. Rory Waterman (Five Leaves Publications, 2015).

'Weddings', 'The Railway Station in Stamford' and 'The Font' originally appeared in *The Fen Dancing* (Red Squirrel Press, 2014).

Contents

Slow Stopping Trains

The Flitting

The Moving Field

for Fiona

Karolles, wrastlynges, or somour games,
Whoso euer haunteþ any swyche shames
Yn cherche, oþer in chercheyerd,
Of sacrylage he may be aferd.

—Robert Mannyng of Brunne
The Dancers of Colbek

Slow Stopping Trains

The Journey

Grantham: 1944
i.m. Charlotte Annie Bodsworth

The long road from the farm was longer then,
the chickens fed, breakfast on the table,
then stopping trains and unfamiliar stations
to Grantham's cobbled market squares.

You came to see your new-born grandchild,
the poet sleeping in his earliest days.
Nothing would have stopped you, a right lass,
livelier than the youngsters in your black shawl.

You died weeks later, as the bluebells came.
'Seeing you,' my father said, a family joke.
The long journey a likelier story.
And mine, in after-years, struggling for words.

You came to see your new-born grandchild,
a day's trip away from Pillar Box Farm,
to make your claim on an unknown future,
plant the seeds of our secret harvest.

Wagon & Horses

Grantham: 1947

At night I hear the revellers in the yard,
soldiers home from war, girls on their arms,
the clink of bottle tops on cobbled stone.
In restless sleep I lead my beer patrol.

They might be back from Napoleon's wars,
the drunken soldiery no longer dead,
horses or a child's dream of horses,
a harmless kind of cavalry charge.

The night is stars and planets wide,
as the yard of the 'Wagon & Horses'
is wide, welcoming the homeless home.
They stumble legless across rough fields,

ghosts of the mud of the Great War,
veterans of Dunkirk's scoured dunes.
In the slap of river water down the road
they hear the frozen waves of German Seas.

And I hear dolls in the darkness talking,
whispering their news of dolls' houses,
gossip like minnows and tiddlers
truer than the morning's raw headlines.

The Stove

i.m. Eleanor Grey

The stove in the sunken classroom
burns coke to a yellow glow,
warming your storyteller's murmur.

St Wulfram's spire chills the room,
graves and gargoyles
grinning to the ravens' croak.

You kept a fireguard round the fire,
reading at the end of each school day:
faraway trees and magic circles,

the gate into the secret garden,
the traveller knocking at the moonlit door.
The stove has been taken away,

and the children who sang in a choir
at the side of your cold grave
have already left the classroom –

where you sit in your old chair,
and the stove burns coke to a yellow glow,
warming your storyteller's murmur.

Belton Park

*In a somer seson, whan softe was the sonne,**
the chauffeur's son showed me the attics,
long empty corridors and servants' rooms,
net curtains blowing at cobwebbed windows.

'They might find us,' is what I wanted to say,
imagining the crack of autumn guns.
'They're away,' he scoffed, reading my mind:
the family, the servants, priests on the run.

In the library, a visitor worked at his books:
a priestly recorder in a Pennyfeather mood,
a yellow waistcoat and hot complexion,
crouched at his words like a smith at the forge.**

In the grounds, under oak and hornbeam,
my father hit the ball to the boundary,
shouting 'Yes!' as he raced for the wickets,
still running when the umpire called for tea.

In a somer seson, whan softe was the sonne,
all that was begun ended. Our brief goodbye
and a wave, then the plane taking off
like a cricketer running for the boundary.

* William Langland, *The Vision of Piers Plowman*

** A friend of the Brownlow family, Evelyn Waugh was a frequent
visitor to Belton House, where he liked to work in the library.

Apples

Isaac Newton in Grantham

Scrumping for windfalls,
you threw an apple in the air,
watching it spin and spiral down,
until it landed on the ground,
    landed elsewhere,
beyond the redbrick orchard walls.

No matter what *elsewhere*,
farms and colleges
held smells of field and court:
the acres of Wultsthorpe green,
    then bitter
fenland cold of Cambridge rain.

At the King's School,
on the 'Wagon & Horses' road,
your ghost-walks were rare,
a schoolboy hoping to see
    the apple fly,
the answer scribbled on the air.

Now I hear voices:
boys scrumping for windfalls,
the Woolsthorpe youngsters on a lark,
while you are far elsewhere,
    like Schrödinger's cat,
your eyes fixed on the stars.

Skater

i.m. Edith Annie Bedford: 1915–1919

We waited for the end of school,
then ran to spin and glide
across a field of ice,
the ghosts of summer cattle grazing
beneath the elms.

                    Set free,
you wouldn't stay to watch,
clenched fingers cold in lambswool gloves,
shivering at the risk of being asked
to share the dance. You ran for home.

Come spring,
the grass caught sun,
freewheeling birds aloft
chasing your shadow beneath the skating elms,
circling free from cold and school room bells.

Fishing

Tiddlers and minnows in the freshwater tub
stank the yard out for days. 'Damned child,'
the spinster next door complained.

How did we catch them? With a rod and net,
dredging the river's fast-flowing water,
leaning out over the edge.

The mud brought them up, churning sunlight.
We must have caught hundreds,
a living graveyard packed tight together,

swimming in the depths of the freshwater tub.
My mother whaled me and sent me to bed,
but not for the smell in the cobbled yard:

she liked to wash her hair in fresh rain water,
fallen like a blessing from the clean skies.
When we moved away, we left the net behind.

Grannie Peacock

The pansies in your garden walked on water
whenever the river drowned the lawn.
Not something you intended.
They planted themselves,

flashes of colour,
real as when you saw the future.
Reading tealeaves was your special promise:
an afternoon spent telling us the future.

When you died,
I thought of them dancing,
the pansies you said were not intended,
flashes of colour turning dark as the waters rose.

Weddings

We were there to sand floors and scrub tiles,
preparing the house for the new bride,
your sister gleaning some kind
of country harvest
from the trick of a kind smile. I ran wild,
beguiled by the pollen-thickened air,
nasturtium wildernesses climbing into tall rooms,
the hot echo of sunlight.

In the garden a sundial told the weather,
and at night, a boy waiting in shadow
led me beneath the limes
to the stream buried in forget-me-nots,
the muddy banks of drowning.
If you looked closely,
a face smiled from the shallows,
trembling with hope in the cold current,
the child unborn of the marriage never to happen.

The Freeze

Winter: 1947

You could walk on the ice
if you had the nerve.
See the world turned upside down:
swans ice-skating instead of flying,
tiddlers frozen in the water,
an abandoned boot
half-drowned.
'You don't go down there,'
my father said, knowing water.
'You'll not be safe.'

My mother rattled pans,
turned the wireless loud,
laughed when the gate slammed.
'They'll be hungry,' she said,
breaking bread into crumbs.
'You don't want them hungry.'
They were hungry,
screeched for the sky,
stumbled off the lumpy ice,
followed us back up the road.

The gate jambed.
Cobbles tricked our feet
on sun-polished snow.
Frost flowered the windows.
We closed the kitchen door,
dropped the catch, froze:
six swans huddled in a clutch,
pecking at the moon,
waiting for the stars to race them
out of the yard with a broom.

The Kitchen Garden

Grantham: 1941

Mrs Pearson's son fetched us the eggs,
a half-dozen for the week
to eke out the rationing regime:
'Don tell they nosy neighbours.
They gets none.' Old Lincolnshire,
from the estate farm.

                He walked me there once,
a country kind of Eden, sunk lanes
and harvest suppers, sunlight on redbrick walls.
He worked the kitchen gardens:
a regular harvest supper
of fruit and vegetables, what flowers
they let grow wild. 'Not weeds,' he scoffed:
'windfalls, survivors.' The leftovers
left from what the kitchen wanted.

The bombers came most days,
passing over the farm on their return home.
He was planting spring lettuce and runner beans.
Turning the earth with an old hoe.
He saw them come. Signed up in the end
waving a red handkerchief
some flyer must have thought meant a warning.
The rabbits were soon after the carrots.
They never found the hoe.

Going Home

Dunkirk 1940
for my father

You never liked the sea,
that churning journey back
upsetting any deeps you'd known
or heard about,

a country boy
with other country boys
used to village ponds
for skating on or washing sheep.

You never talked.
Gunmetal grey or green
hid roots too deep to share,
dug up by toddler me –

'Tell me, tell me' –
playing soldier ghosts
with friends you'd seen thrown
overboard like bait into the sea.

The nurses on the ward
heard words I'd never heard:
'Home, home!' cried from a deep
you'd crossed alone.

Belonging

Harvest Supper: Kirkby Green

You don't belong until the beck has doused you,
a stepping-stone journey across the river
on stones meant to keep your feet dry.

I told you the story. Made things clear.
Each harvest supper a candlelight feast,
the *Book of Common Prayer* and a real presence,

then the village hall where families meet,
dance to a grandfather playing an accordion.
But no light outside to carry you over.

You choose the bridge and reach the other side.
I tumble in, as you turn and walk away,
eager to find the warmth and light inside.

St Edith

for Patricia McCarthy

There is no village where St Edith lies:
Coates-by-Stow an empty field
and copse of trees,
the racketing of crows the only choir.

In barley fields,
Cromwell's ghostly riders clatter by,
the chancel, nave and bellcote
crouched in frosted fear.

Where children used to play,
old women weep
for treasures lost on dusty shelves,
relics sold for gold.

The farm has gone.
The priest has left his beads.
The Corpus Christi guild's long closed.
Still, the lady knows:

above the rood screen's loft
a painted figure smiles:
warm light on wooden panelling,
rose windows broken rainbows.

Guy Fawkes

Humber Estuary: 1955

The last thing our Guy Fawkes will see
is the sea coming in to rescue him.
But the sea won't reach. The rockets
and Catherine wheels will reach,

but the tide is too low to douse a fire.
Shrivelled to penny eyes and shells for teeth,
his ashes will drift to the estuary,
his wide mouth leak the oils and tars

of Sheffield's industrial froth.
Push-netters shrimping the shallows
might have helped if they had hearts,
but they're ranters and levellers to a man.

Everybody loves a bonfire.
Everybody loves to see Guy Fawkes burned.
The crowds will pay sixpence for fresh crab
and shrimps in brown paper bags.

The last thing our Guy Fawkes will see
is the cocklers and inshore fishermen,
warm in tarred oilskins and sou'westers,
pretending they are boys again,

shouting for the death of the straw man,
the fire of belief in their eyes,
the fists of the future in their hands,
a dance of screaming crowds in the sea.

The Floods

for Frank Priest: 1953

There have been winter floods before,
but your loss eddies round us,
like a shrimp netter's dross,
caught up by fishermen on a freak tide.

Amusement mocks the promenade,
where sea-salted signs creak in the sun
and loud arcades and palaces of fun
preach empty ruined sermons.

A broken jetty reaches for the sea,
the fingers of a hand spread out and blackening,
the lugworm runnelled sands
a shifting grave of junk and beachcombers.

Here mermaid's purse and brittle star embrace,
the river buoys in tolling funeral dance,
an offering of meaning lighting stars
until dawn's ache unravels meaning's sham.

There have been winter floods before,
but tiding on a wash of herring gulls,
your silence wakes to meet the sea,
as winter shores meet nothing's blank stare.

Laurel and Hardy

Palace Music Hall, Grimsby: March 1954
for Keith Hutson

Stan Laurel was engaged to a local lass,
so they came to the Palace Music Hall,
bringing magic into weary lives with
the Blue Ridge Mountains of Virginia

on the trail of the lonesome pine.
Nicole & Keble were the first act,
then Derek Rosaire and his Wonder Horse,
Betty Kaye with her Pekinese Pets,

the Keefe Brothers and Annette.
The seats were 4/6d, a month's pocket money.
I sat in rows of gold and garish decoration,
but there were fleas in my hair when we left,

and my mother said fleas gave you polio,
like Ralf Betts in our class who wore callipers
to protect his withering legs, but still danced
a slow shine shuffle for Stan and Oliver.

Tennyson at Mablethorpe

(1)

This is where he walked,
bare-legged on tussocked dunes
or paddling in the sea,
the tug of wind against his face
smoothing frazzled nerves,
furrowed frown. Hallam knew.
Walked the same dunes,
dark wraith in poet's mind,
cold as German Seas.

(2)

I walk here too,
white sands at low tide
runnelled by the moon's turn,
the lugworm's dance.
All memory frowns,
peopling barren dunes,
setting foreshores mourning
and seagulls churning waves,
for me, for you.

Somersby

The church squats like a grey toad,
huddled on the escarpment's edge,
waiting for a mighty claw from heaven.
When we open the door, the cold hurts:

black pews and a blacker heaven
hidden among yews and leaking stones;
the hollow eye of the collecting bowl.
But that voice crying 'Father, forgive them',

is the wind, surely, in the ugly tower,
guilt singing its familiar blackmail?
We stand, rigid, in the empty porch,
words raining from coloured glass,

pain leaping from the saintly histories.
In leafless branches, ghosts weep,
children of our soiled imagination:
the taut farmers and parish councillors,

angry women with their sullen lives.
Outside, in sun, the yews creak.
The sundial spreads its green corrosion.
Through frozen hedgerows, time leaks.

In Memoriam

Folded in mist,
the church bells peal,
the patient snow a holly wreath for grief.

The moon is hidden,
climbing the limestone hill,
the village choir a clamour of new life.

We cannot stay,
trespassers on hallowed ground,
tracing spring flowers on glass thick with frost.

I walk the hills,
the blue ache of the Wolds,
as lonely in my years as you in yours.

Folded in mist,
the church bells peal,
tolling the long yearn to walk away.

Sons and Lovers

Paul and Miriam in Mablethorpe

I couldn't bend the sea to my way.
'It don't bend,' the fishermen reckoned,
baiting the lines for the day's catch,
whistling the devil out of the water.

Great sweeps of sand send back the light,
no noise but the sound of the sea,
marram grass whispering in the wind,
fortune-telling songs of the drowned.

And at dusk, a brilliant orange moon.
The *Bride of Enderby* showed the way:
sea meadow, white barley and yellow oats,
lamplight at the windows to draw the bats.

Reckon that. From the rim of sandhills,
dark fen-meadow, see the tide break,
the embarrassed lovers running free,
crossing the plank bridge to hurry home.

Paul's mother was mad as mine,
devouring-angel in a white disguise,
hearing the tide but ignoring its warning,
the flooding dykes with their talk of water.

The Railway Station in Stamford

This was not Adlestrop,
and the girl waiting on the platform,
wearing a blue summer dress,
had never heard of Edward Thomas.

A quiet platform certainly,
but far from Oxfordshire or Gloucestershire,
and the poet Edward Thomas,
who may have visited, but never stopped.

Only the birds
reckon the same memories,
racketing above the station clock
as if Adlestrop should be remembered everywhere.

The Western Wynde

John Taverner 1490–1545*

I walk in sunlit Christ Church meadows,
the skies not Lincolnshire –
the grazing cattle and unfamiliar deer –
a winter afternoon not seen before.

Strange voices seem to chill the air,
The Western Wynde unwinding
in my ear: the river's rhythm,
polyphony of crows.

I walk in sunlit Christ Church meadows,
the choirmaster far from home,
where ghosts listen to country stories,
children haunt the buttercross.

Now music sings to fetch the past:
a girl dancing in the May dawns,
a boy snowballing the Lincolnshire trees.
The choirmaster knows his part.

So choristers and college clerkes
rehearse in music the fields
and lanes he didn't want to leave,
far parish of the aching heart.

* John Taverner was born in Tattershall, Lincolnshire.
  He was choirmaster at Tattershall Collegiate Church
  and at Cardinal – subsequently Christ Church –
  College, Oxford.

The Flitting

i.m. John Clare

'Thou tellest my flittings; put my tears into thy bottle:
are not these things noted in thy book?'

—Psalm 56
The Book of Common Prayer (1662)

Note on Text

In trying to write about John Clare's life and work, and given the controversial history of the published and manuscript poetry and prose, I have tried to honour his spelling, punctuation and use of dialect, whilst leaving space for twenty-first century sympathies and understanding.

The Schoolroom

Glinton Vestry: 1805

I went to learn,
a cabbage kind of prince,
and nobbut soft for books and girls,

sweet Mary Joyce
my only classroom friend.
That weren't just books when she said no.

I left with nowt,
John Seaton's pupil lost for words,
Old Moore's the better almanac for poets.

So every winter night
our once unlettered hearth was broomed,
a catch-as-can scratch schoolroom,

with books and pens
for scribbling nouns and verbs,
and Pilgrim chasing Crusoe down the lanes.

I went to learn,
came back to be a ghost,
John Seaton's earnest pupil at his words.

But Seaton died,
and Mary Joyce moved on,
my classroom dreams old spiderwebs and dust.

Zig Zag and *Cinderella*
was all time left,
a giant beanstalk reaching for the skies.

John Seaton was a schoolteacher who ran a makeshift schoolroom in the vestry of the parish church at Glinton. **Zig Zag** refers to the nineteenth-century children's story entitled 'The Man with a Long Nose'.

World's End

Where is the end of the world? –
a clown's question not asked by the learnd,
but asked by me,
no parson's answer singing like a bird.

I knew they got things wrong,
orison's beckoning finger
like sunlight falling off a tree,
the promise of the yellow furze stretching

to dawn's buzzing chittering answer.
I knew at the edge of the world,
I would look down
and see the secret of beginnings,

like heaven shining in a beck's cold waters.
So eagerly I wanderd on,
wild birdsong leaving no place for fears,
my wonder seeking walking

walking me far from home.
But home ent just a thatch and kitchen,
lamplight and fire.
I walked myself out of my own knowledge.

The birds and flowers seemd to forget me.
The sun seemd to be new though
the sky still touched the ground.
Night crept on like a poacher,

hedge crickets whispering to the village ghosts,
mice nimbling and twittering.
I hurried then. I ran.
Stumbled.

And when chance brought me home,
back to my own fields,
the village was up and out hunting,
hunting for me,

the lost child lost wandering,
my parents fallen into grief.
I knew then my own orisons.
I knew the questions not to be answered.

learnd: Clare used contractions frequently but not consistently
orison's: Clare's spelling of horizon's, though he would presumably
have been familiar from church services with the liturgical meaning:
a prayer

The Year Without a Summer

1816

No crops here in a drere summer,
mists fogs rains,
sad wi'out sun wi'out fun
wi'out harvest dancing and beer.

The bluebell woods sing spring's about,
as wood-pigeon white brings cooing
of blue day's tune,
a hint of summer's hum.

Yet summer's slow coming.
There's no fruit. No corn.
No harvest supper 'cept swing riots,
troops tredding the ploughboys down.

Nowt new in that
the harvest men reckon,
now childerns' stomachs rattle agen,
clamouring complaint.

But protest don't get heard.
Barred gate is new,
carpented in Norberry,
carted here on greed's right.

Bosses say:
you can eat the shavings,
imagine grass tastes like bread.
Some on us hev to.

Old Jacob Lea down drowned lane,
told us the end is coming.
His words 'ent music enough for song,
and nobody 'ent listening.

1816: known as the year without a summer, because of climatic changes caused by the Mount Tambora volcano
Norberry: Northborough

The Pettichap

There's worlds built in shells –
egg shells, pooty shells,
homes built to last,
'till caught by eye of passersby.

We go for hedgerows, woodlands, roots of trees,
our hiding places born as rights.
But rights don't last,
our being in the world forgot

and trampled down,
fenced off.
The pettichap's the same,
no lawyer's fee to stake her claim.

She builds beside the track,
brown earth, green grass to hide her flight,
her chosen home
a rounded female space.

When nesting boys disturb her eggs,
her world has gone.
Mine too,
struggling to make a nesting place

where strangers
plough the heath, dam the stream,
cut the village willow down,
sell our dreams.

pettichap: chiffchaff
pooty: snail

Skaiting

for Abegail Morley

There was a field where frost's come,
cobwebs white, grass white,
ground gone,
overnight,

new mirror for dazzling sun.
Now skaiters waltz – laugh – cry –
skreek like magpie
passing by.

I skait across my mind,
tek falls no skaiter understands,
read winter words
in red sky.

Sit on farm gate
that fences heaven round,
no trespasses allowed for larks
or rabbit pie.

There was a field where frost's come,
new owner of the heath,
pasture ground,
rainbows in the free sky.

skaiting: skating
skreek: shriek, scream

Cawdymawdy

A bird might fly
as high as clouds or sun,
white cawdymawdy
caught in dazzling light,
hartsomely bland
to come so far inland
for grub our fields supply,
seawrack and shellfish left behind.

We can try,
but that's not meant for us,
earthbound and tied, trussed.
Our feet were meant
for tredding down,
or being trod down. Not flight.
In woodland quiet,
we speak the creak of rooted trees.

cawdymawdy: herring gull
hartsomely: with good heart or cheer, blithely

I Am

'I am, yet what I am, none cares or knows.'
—John Clare

A taproom weaver show'd me heaven,
Thomson's *Seasons* his drunken fun,
my heart lurching like a cart of hay.
I knew he laughed, mocked the lines,

blank verse or rhyme a thing for hymns
or ballad singers' cheapest trash,
chapel mornings or taproom brags.
I had to own such verses. I had to sing.

Teazed the shillings off my father,
and walked to Stamford in summer rain.
The lowering High Street stood deserted,
bookseller and printer away from home.

'You never 'eard o' Sundays?'
a crowd of grinning childern clowned.
I stole a day off work. Lost that job.
Then sat in leafy Burghly sun,

rhyming the blue shine of heaven,
reckless in summer morning sunlight
where skylarks weaved and spelled
their own wild stories. The world to tell.

Thomson's Seasons: James Thomson's poem *The Seasons* went through 250 editions between 1790 and 1830. In the summer of 1806, a Helpston weaver showed a fragment of the poem to the thirteen-year-old Clare.

Mouldiwarp

Blind moles shove agen the dark
like poets through earth's tunnels.
Milton knew that: darkness visible, lost wife,

but hearing woodpecker's sweeing flight,
jay's warning chatter,
sod's riddle.

Truth is clap of wood pigeon's wing,
sound of cuckoo far and near,
near and far. Echoes wrapt.

mouldiwarp: mole
sweeing: swooping

Take Your Own Trundle

Crows bate me,
scarecrow boy unbrunt
by glabbering lords,
ladies' whews,

I shut my mind to crows
preachin' pews
noise
the clatterin' hawks chasin' food.

Mary's watchet eyes
watch me with sad surprise,
old cart carting love
to paradise.

take your own trundle: go your own way
bate: harass
unbrunt: unhindered by
glabbering: chattering
whews: the cry of birds, or imitating the cry of birds
Mary: Mary Joyce, Clare's childhood sweetheart
watchet: light blue

Byron

I could hev bin Byron I s'pose,
but perched on a wrong bough,
out nesting instead of learning,
following ploughs.

Skies used to be blue.
I reckon somebody painted they grey.
You know the way blue
drizzles to grey?

Reckoning church windows,
all the critters
in Noah's Ark. That had done me.
Telling stories.

I am a man,
despite what they say.
I eat bread and cheese,
tek a horn of ale in the Blue Bell.

He wouldn't have liked fen country.
Too many dykes. Reeds.
Taproom talkers,
Methodists mostly. Tinkers.

I could hev bin Byron I s'pose,
but the weather
was agin me.
Perched on a wrong bough.

The Fancy

Until fame's lick
I rambled on unkend,
my nightly fight
a dozen sweaty rounds
to tek three peacock gallants out.

Now gamblers
watch me dance,
midsummer prance on lawns,
grass meant to feed
the cat that's gypsey-black as soot.

Light-stepping
weeds – moss – fuss
I dodge and partner fame.
I am the man
who knocked Jack Randall out –

though Hazlitt says
sweet prosers canna fight.
I hear the cheering crowds,
the lords and ladies
betting least and worst of all.

the fancy: bare-knuckle boxing
unkend: unrecognized
Jack Randall: famous bare-knuckle boxer, one of the identities
Clare adopted in his illness
canna: cannot

They Are Selling Our Fields

They are selling our fields.
Be selling streams and willows soon,
the oldest trees heaven made for climbing.

Our bruises they say are ours,
earned from falling. Shouldn't climb.
Nettles sting. Ground's hard.

Scabs are our deals.
Nowt to do with them.
They are selling our fields.

I reckon it's lies.
So a cuckoo
gets to own the thrush's home.

Only larks stay free, living in skies.
I will live in skies.
Eat clouds. Drink rain.

We Never Met

i.m. John Keats

We never met,
missed by chance,
though you more comfortable
where poets meet than me,
farmyards and fields my close familiars.

Then death looked by,
you at sea, me back at home.
Taylor said you wrote:
my Images from Nature
not called by any living Sentiment.

Best criticism I ever received,
words not to be thrown away.
I read your Chaucer, Taylor's own copy.
So poets to poets,
across a much wider sea.

Pleughing

The sheep-track through the thistly pasture
mimes my own way. Sunday mawkin
avoiding preacher's pews.

There's spangled dragon-flies on my mind,
darting swallows, ripening grain.
I ache for girls,

throw me sen down, flower of the meadow,
poesy's fellow, eking rimes.
What's words

to wild geese scudding
or city sidestreets full of swollen mouths,
seeping eyes?

I pitch the clover's copper blossom
in jostling lanes and gaudy lights
that blind my eyes,

leave aching bones
to rue the pleughing nights,
and crab-juice swallowing moans.

Then tramper
weary home like shanny village girl
fust kissed and left alone,

that witching fatal taste of sin
where scarlet head-aches strew the road,
and death begins.

sen: self
eking: stretching out
pleughing: ploughing, slang for having sex
wrecky: fragments
tramper: tramp
shanny: shy
witching: bewitching
scarlet head-aches: poppies

To Hear the Wooden Cuckoo Sing

Our Helpston wags tell tales of strangers,
slow-witted lads from other towns,
traipsing round to hear the wooden cuckoo sing.
I think of that in fancy Lunnon town,
bigger than Norberry but nowt brighter,
'cept for lights, flash clothes, bold stares,
posh table manners worn to make us know
we're out of place, down here, or anywhere.
But I don't hear the wooden cuckoo sing
whatever place I'm in, alehouse or field,
theatre or quack's asylum. I hear the clouds,
see the stars, listen to the moon talking.
I know a place that's mine, and that's not here.

Lunnon: London
Norberry: Northborough, where Helpston locals thought
the slow-witted went to hear the wooden cuckoo sing

Wopstraw Clack

He liked Mary, folks say. Talked to her.
Gawped in Seaton's classroom.
Lost work dreaming tales better not dreamt.

Liked trees too, willows 'specially,
the way they leaned out over water,
reaching for t'other side. Daft, some folk said.

He allus liked Mary.
Followed her home, though she wouldn't listen.
His youthful crush, blushy youngen.

Her fether knew better.
Martha was the one he married.
Called her Patty. His good woman.

He hadn't heard Mary died.
Went walking home, flitting asylum.
His other wife on his mind. Woody nightshade.

wopstraw: country bumpkin
clack: chatter, gossip
Mary: Mary Joyce, Clare's childhood sweetheart
youngen: youngster
Martha: Martha Turner, Clare's wife, known by him as Patty

Blue Devils

Thin goblin shadows with sorcerer eyes
traipse behind my starving skeleton,
aching for Lunnon crowds,
the company of my own kind,
poets and talkers,
fine gals,
not sneering wopstraws,
poverty's jeers,
poesy my ride to idiocy.
How wandering pains gripe me,
blistering chills, sweat of tears.
I am alone. I am the only one of my kind.
Nobody wants the gifts I bring,
the wordy woods and rambling miles,
fields where the fieldfares follow,
not traipsing but flying high.

Lunnon: London
wopstraw: country bumpkin

Send Him Away

I crouch in the corner like a caught beast,
badger or fox hearing the horn,
knowing the kill will come,
waiting release.

He scribbles his notes in urgent prose,
words of care as cold as stone:
Send him away, for his own sake,
for his woman's sake,

leave his childern, leave his home ...
my writing 'in the fit' my wife's evidence,
my freedom with fists
his pretend care.

Cattle are given as much chance.
Boxers for the prize at the summer fair.
But the prize for poesy is an idiot's crown.
I am food for village gossips' chelp.

I am but what I am no wopstraw cares.
I crouch in the corner like a caught beast,
as I see you agree, nod to agree,
turning away as I leave.

He scribbles his notes in urgent prose: Dr Fenwick Skrimshire
was the Peterborough doctor who looked after Clare between
1820 and his committal to the Northampton General Lunatic
Asylum in 1841.
in the fit: Clare's own description, in a letter of April 1820,
of his periods of rapid, prolific poetic composition
chelp: gossip
wopstraw: country bumpkin

I Stood By Your Cot

I stood by your cot
when it come time to leave,
to say goodbye.

You were asleep.
Best, mebbe.
Too many tears if I'd stayed.

Too many when I'd gone,
I reckon.
Nobody wrote to say.

I allus loved my childern.
Reckoned the fields
Eden,

where they could play.
Nobody listened.
Cared.

I have lost what I loved
the most,
taken away.

Or given, mebbe,
when it came time to leave,
to say goodbye.

They have the words,
written legal.
But not the poetry.

In 1837, John Clare was committed to Matthew Allen's private asylum
in Essex. It was after escaping Matthew Allen's Essex asylum in 1841
that he was committed to Northampton General Lunatic Asylum.

The Flitting

24th July 1841

Two wives I have,
iffen folk say no,
law say no,
feeble brain imagines.

I've walked these miles,
bramble, hazard,
carters' wiles,
a gypsey crawl

to find
a home in Mary's smile.
And still I reckon,
sing love tunes:

huswife and bedwife,
to bicker over moons;
a harvest supper
wi wooden spoons.

'Touched,'
the neighbours snigger.
I whistle rhythms
nobbut fools chose.

And walk at night,
nimbling poacher's ways,
sleep on clover trusses,
chew grass 'cos

fish gone, game gone,
no trespasses
allowed
now fields and common closed.

I chew tobacco too,
then swallow,
no lucifers to light my pipe,
smoke fumes enew.

Two wives I have,
acrost bare fields of stubble,
no pastoral views,
childern learned to reddle.

I walk
where wind whips elms:
frozed night,
red gypsey hat for warmth or trouble.

I walk
where Eden used to be,
haymaking games
a game for saucey drovers.

Then Patty
says me home.
Sweet Mary died.
And how can I forget?

nimbling: moving nimbly
reddle: riddle
enew: enough

In the Porch

1841–1864

Tobacco for my pipe,
a rite for an old feller,
leaning in the church porch.

Bells still rime us nowt,
fields and copse
allus my choice.

I have aches
for company these days
that had poets and fine prosers,

Hazlitt and Lamb,
Mr Taylor
when he wurnt feeling down.

John Keats
wrote me a letter,
sailing for a far shore.

I blow smoke shrouds
as once blew words,
neither making things better.

Hev you seen Mary?
Her smile was my home.
They say she died three year ago.

Patty is my home now,
though she don't visit.
You can't sing that in church choirs.

I have aches for bones,
that once made lasses grateful.
But nobody listens.

During his long years in Northampton Lunatic Asylum, Clare was given considerable freedom, and was often to be seen sitting quietly for hours at a time in the portico of All Saints' Church, always with his tobacco, sometimes with his notebook.

The Fiddler

I am a fiddler
waiting for the next funeral,
a straw bear
dancing with hounds in a bear pit.

The gypseys
know my game,
the bare-knuckle fighter
who knows how to strip a deer,

roast deer for dear
travellers,
sitting round the fires,
fiddling tunes nobody hears.

John Clare's Will

'I wish to lye on the North side the Church yard just about the
middle of the ground were the Morning and Evening sun can
linger the longest on my Grave I wish to have a rough unhewn
stone something in the form of a mile Stone so that the playing
boys may not break it in their heedless pastimes with nothing more
on it then this Inscription:

> I desire that no date be
> inserted there on as I wish
> it to live or dye with my
> poems and other writings
> which if they have merit
> with posterity it will and
> if they have not it is not
> worth preserving.'

The Moving Field

Nutting

'Then up I rose,
And dragged to earth both branch and bough, with crash
And merciless ravage.'
—Wordsworth

They built the hangars on farming land
where winter wheat and skylarks reigned
regardless of the bright imperial sun.
In silos, gods of war hid beneath the ground.

From hawthorn hedge and tree we watched
the monthly testings: four-minute warnings
telling the end of nature's harvest round
in alphabets of war. Birds paused.

Trees waited. A combine harvester stood by.
The jeeps and vans of military police
patrolled our minds. 'No trespassers,'
the commandant's command. No spies allowed.

A mile away, we dragged horse chestnut
branches down, a scattering of leaves
baptising hedge school saws: the drovers' roads,
the fields of speedwell trodden under plough.

The Tulip Farm

Spalding Flower Festival 1971

The tulip fields dazzle the sun,
a red carpet carpeting day and night,
confusing weasel and rabbit
like a red traffic light.

Lovers think the moon bleeds,
so close their eyes to make love.
If the tulip fields were green
it would be all right,

a welcome for the harvesters,
the casual khaki army
preparing for the flower parade,
a circus of dewed petals

stitched into gargoyle shapes:
angels and princesses, mermaids,
dolphins on a turtle's back,
a festival of artificial candles.

At night,
when the parade is over,
the farm sinks back into owl cry,
the feasting of weasel and baby rabbit.

Stubble

They're shooting pheasants in Fry's fields,
guns over the woods
and boots treading stubble,
indifferent voices crying dogs to heel.

What's left after harvest pocks the ground
where the winter sheep
are put to graze.
This is the autumn before the freeze:

leftover windfalls
falling from the frost-rimed trees,
harvest suppers and a dance in Fry's fields,
a thanksgiving service of grace and chance.

White Out

Winter 1962–1963

Trekking across deep snow,
lanes and ditches painted white,
we go to the rescue like heroes
in a Biggles adventure.

You have tennis rackets
tied to your shoes.
My fingers are cold
carrying the packages of food.

Snow flurries turn to snow,
and we can't see
the telegraph poles
marching down into the village.

There seems
a long way to go,
but tiredness makes us feel warm,
as the crows in the sky wait.

When the Americans Came

USAF Hemswell: North Lincolnshire 1962

When the Americans came,
they didn't take to our gardens:
the apple orchard smelling of wild garlic,
foxgloves growing among the runner beans.

'Do you have vampires around here?'
a visitor from Carolina asked me.
It was a shambles, Wilfred knew that,
nodding wisely as though apologising

for the ill manners of King George,
the clematis purple in the thatched roofing.
But come the *softe sonne*,
there are oxlips in Fry's woods,

forget-me-nots in the shallow stream,
lettuce and spring onions for a salad.
It's certain that fine women eat
A crazy salad with their meat*

I tried to tell them. But they weren't women,
and didn't care to listen to a boy.
They preferred the red rosehips
we used for making wine.

Danced outside the village church
round the maypole Jack Parnham made.
Now they're gone,
the wild garlic has returned.

* W. B. Yeats, 'A Prayer for my Daughter'

The Police House

USAF Hemswell: 1959

1 Callers

Arrivals for the camp called every day,
officers and servicemen, their wives too,
coming to register as aliens.
The daily parade was a blue-silk nuisance:

me upstairs with *A Portrait of the Artist*,
my mother dollying the week's clothes,
my father scare-crowing the garden.
He struggled into uniform, muttering oaths,

searching for the keys to the locked office,
station and home in the same building.
'Can they not wait until the morning!
Can they not sign up when they go to town!'

But we were aliens too:
me from the east coast fishing grounds –
my mother from Sheffield's Brightside slums –
my father from a farm in the Methodist south

where he had never known a Catholic priest,
just the Kerry labourers hired for harvest –
where he had never seen a black face,
didn't know the word 'negro'.

The Catholic chaplain had visited before,
knew the weight of the word stranger.
An older man. Wiser. 'Different in the war,'
he smiled. Something my father understood.

The black sergeant was from Tennessee:
signed the forms with an expensive Parker,
shook my father's hand when he stood to leave.
In the kitchen, I saw my father using soap and water.

2 The Greylag Goose

The greylag goose is a loner, often flying with the Canada geese.

The police house had an office and a cell,
handcuffs hanging behind the door,
a blue sign at the garden gates saying
Lincolnshire Police in gold letters.

Like Canada Geese the aliens arrived,
American transports in English fields,
burning the speedwell that salved our pain.
The birds migrated. The men came to stay.

On night patrol, my father used his bike,
his blue lamp warning poachers he was near.
The farmers paid in sacks of fresh produce.
The poachers left whatever they couldn't sell.

'You don't carry a gun!' a Master Sergeant said,
surprised. 'Don't need one,' my father lied,
home from an afternoon of shooting game.
'All personnel newly landed to register,'

the southern Baptist commandant advised,
MPs on white-stave duty to make it happen.
Their guardhouse cells were crammed with boys,
Carlsberg Special Naafi subsidised,

cheaper still in the American PX.
That's why the local farm girls loved GIs.
Who'd walk or ride a bike with Cadillacs
and blue silk uniforms to tempt the game?

My father signed the forms with black biro,
carving his signature into history's game,
Canada Geese migrating foreign skies.
I was the Greylag Goose, lost on thermal heat.

3 Legal Fictions

The gifts were from grateful farmers:
sacks of potatoes for the store,
eggs until we owned our own chickens,
free harvest suppers left in the dark.

My father went cycling every night,
watching for poachers in Fry's woods.
When the pheasants arrived,
my mother refused to touch them.

She thought they were bribes.
'Home made jam would be more useful,'
she said, in charge in the kitchen,
proud of her blue Yorkshire tiles ...

while my father route-marched the stars,
following the screech of night-owls,
the stink of game in poachers' kitchens,
his lamp warm as a summer glow-worm.

Camp Perimeter

for Trisha: October 1962

I bring you Ezra Pound's poems,
sliding foxily the fox lanes,
cruising

the six o'clock dawn bristle.
But your father opens the door,
stiffening for duty,

ready for war.
The camp is no place for poets.
Military mowers cut the grass.

The air is nuclear.
'Traitor!' flares from his mouth. 'Mad!'
I run for shelter.

'Love,' I want to shout. 'Love.'
The dawn's red lunatic.

To Speke of Wo that is in Mariage

The Wolds smoke in a limestone haze:
sunlight on lichened gravestones,
swifts climbing their hot chimney.

We walked here after the wedding,
wood nymph – satyr – wanting for light,
heart broiling in the crimped air,

like the hair of women on electric tongs,
a frizzling of regret turning to stone.
I think we were meant to leave,

market towns and tired farms
breeding a redbrick Methodist gloom,
chapels and solicitors' offices

where they sign the certificates
guaranteeing a quick electric death,
herds of light shuffling to squalid darkness.

All Saints

They're closing the church down,
though the crocuses on the graves don't know that,
the crows circling the squat tower.
In the *Domesday Book* they say Helmeswelle,
a village of thirty-nine dwellings, hidden away.
They should have done it when the maypole went,
the end of praying and dancing.
The shop's closing down. The pub's still open,
but selling wine to American tourists,
a farm labourer's stories the only souvenirs.
We don't know who'll maintain the graveyard,
answer the tourists' questions.
They often know more about the church than us:
have the brochure, checked the internet.
They're interested, though they don't pray.
Leave unwanted change in the porch.
The crocuses on the graves are much photographed,
though they will soon be out of season.
The crows don't know what all the fuss is about.

The Willow Tree

for Steven Matthews

You could go underground.
   Hide in the hollow trunk
   of a willow tree,*
seek roots rich with earth
to heal the nettle wounds.

Or climb for endless blue:
   a cloudless afternoon
   where skylarks rule,
their challenging cry
a music carolling for you.

The hollow tree holds it all:
   fast-flowing waters
   of the wide river,
acres of stinging weeds
hiding Arthur's magic sword.

Only the sword was real,
   hammered for war
   in 1914,
first lost then forgotten,
no scabbard to tell its story.

Some kind of lovers' fall?
   A promise given,
   a word kept,
white feathers for a tryst
meant to swerve from death.

All life is rise and fall.
   The sword still shivers
   from the dark:
children playing games,
old men telling old stories.

* *'Hide in the hollow trunk*
  of the willow tree.'
  —Seamus Heaney, 'Oracle'

The Font*

for Rachael

The words round the font are before your time,
before my time, a baptism in history
we weren't expecting.
Stained windows colour the rhyme:

Pater Noster, Ave Maria, Criede,
chiselled for a greystone reminder,
a stern mnemonic
to *Leren the childe yt is need.*

You reach for a rainbow of ancient sunlight,
a cobweb's dance, and a cobweb dancing,
carolling our need.
Outside, the threshing elms ignite.

* The font in St George's, Bradley, Lincolnshire survived the
  Reformation and is mentioned in Eamon Duffy's *The Stripping
  of the Altars.*

The Rainbow

Will and Anna Brangwen in Lincoln Cathedral

The angel pointing to a word in a book
shows us the way: Anna and Will
on their fraught journey,
The Rainbow's glimpse of love's horizon.

This is the genuine English School:
the Angel Choir a wonder in stone,
the shafts of light
lifting souls to heaven.

In stiff-leafed foliage and carved bosses
bright fragments of colour
leap from the Rose windows,
tablets of wisdom from the *Wisdom* tomes.

But the girl doesn't want her soul's flight,
pale light lifting
her love to heaven.
She wants her lover with outspread wings

pointing to a word in a book unwritten,
the Lincoln Imp
a craftsman's gargoyle,
mocking the architect's grand design.

The Badger

I grunt for a wisdom men don't know:
grubs and worms and fallen fruit,
trees where I dig for roots,
a badger's kingdom. Night is my time.

I can fight the sticks & stones of boys,
men with poison and brass-tongued tunes,
the hounds baying daylight's moon.
Time has more chance than guns.

Time's a different kind of hunt.
The mobs need beer, steel knives
and wooden staves, fires to fight fear
as I turn and bare my bone teeth.

Time doesn't mind. Likes to creep.
Or waits round corners no one finds.
Time has heavier stones than boys.
Sharper sticks.

I grunt for a wisdom men don't know,
the drunken crowd, the clown on horse,
the human animal wanting fun.
I bait them all. Catch all.

The Translator

I walk to the end of the lane,
and winter goes with me,
greying the white skies
like snow gathering in a hare's eyes.

Geese flock to the blue Wolds.
If I could write the fox
in the hedgerows,
that might be a story worth telling,

but the fox slips from view,
hearing the remote cry
of the hounds,
the clamour of a vixen's hunger.

So I sit beside the river,
in a story I do not recognise:
the gossip of unfriendly crows,
the chatter of the stream's pebbles –

and know
I cannot write the meadows,
the stumbling of a scarecrow stranger
as the deer frisk their surprise.

Ancestors

They were born here:
had birth, marriage and death
written on the local stone;
had years, singing harvest home.

The bells muffle their song:
farmers and steeplejacks,
carriers and never-kissed girls,
the young on their way to heaven.

They did not choose the prayers:
a music of loss and leaving
turning grief to tearless stone,
yellow lichen round love's words.

But out of this,
and a winter afternoon,
in a graveyard, they attempt the stars,
like the snow, falling through silence.

Old Jeffrey

Epworth Rectory: 1716
for David Cooke

Something happened here:
I feel my heart strangely warmed,
defying Old Jeffrey's blaring horn,
the poltergeist railing against heaven.

Upstairs, the thundering continues,
drowning family prayers
as Epworth moves
to the centre of the earth,

Blake's children
chained to their machines,
skylarks rivetting roofs
to the Lord's perfected metre.

Old Jeffrey moans on the stairs,
railing and hymning the family's doom,
blowing his invisible horn
to warn of the shadows in the gloom.

I feel my heart strangely warmed.
Lie naked through wintry nights.
I am a brand plucked out of the fire.
You will see a brand plucked out of the fire.

The Moving Field

'Then all at once there ran out a horde of rats.'
—Langland
The Vision of Piers Plowman

You leant on the gate and talked of dowsing:
the poet's walk across hidden water,
the hand guiding what the heart seeks.
'Cedar's best,' you said, 'my way of thinking.'

I prefer looking where I know what I'll find.
Not maps, but known landscapes:
streams, copses, familiar valleys;
the astronomer's way with stars.

'But you can never tell with fields,'
you went on, nodding out of some memory.
You saw a field once, moving in sunlight,
like a river surging for the estuary.

'It was rats, travelling across country.
Thousands of them, in a swarm,
devouring a whole year's harvest.
Nobody could ever have predicted that,

though it got to be common, after the war.
You could do nothing. Just stand and watch.'
We do nothing, in a fen twilight.
Two strangers, talking about dowsing.

Then

North Lincolnshire: 1959–1963
for Alison Brackenbury

I had to kill them when it was time to go,
take my leave and catch the stopping train.
Rhode Island Reds they were,
kept for the eggs and kitchen table.
We tarred the wounds of the flock's victim,
locked the hutch at night with twined wire.
If we left the gate open, two followed us
up the garden. One dared the kitchen,
sitting for a photograph on my shoulder.
The other stayed in the yard outside.
I had to kill them when it was time to leave.
The one sitting on my knee was the tamest,
used to pecking seed from warm hands.
She seemed surprised, finding no seed,
not worrying I was going to break her neck.
My father had to fetch the farmer. I cried.
All twelve were gone in a heaven's blink,
a grubby fiver, then biscuits and a cup of tea.
We sold them for the table. Our own stood empty.
Too poor a food for us in pheasant season.

To East Coker*

i.m. Wilfred and Emily Holmes

The deep lane unwinds
while the van passes
like a sundial moving backwards,
a dazzling glimpse of time.

I have saved these flashes
instead of photographs:
Wilfred and Emily
laughing in a cottage garden;

children freewheeling
in the school-free air;
a neighbour collecting
simples from the orchard.

So the mind dwells delicately
on the glistening surface,
like a butterfly
on a blown curtain.

You touched me into dance
and a Latin carolling.
Fifty years,
and you waltz with me everywhere.

* T.S. Eliot, *East Coker*

The Dancers of Colbek

i.m. Norman Francis Blake

Karolles, wrastlynges, or somour games
set me jigging with first words,
the Dancers of Colbek leading the way.
They felt neither snow nor rain,
keeping the priest from the sacred runes.
This is fairyland, despite what the sermons say.
They knew what dancing in church would mean:
the doors locked, the altar denied,
the magic of wafer and wine taken away,
safe behind the rood screen where the ghosts hide.
There are bones buried beyond the graves,
where dancers they've never known
are forced to lie, scattered on unholy ground.
You wrote to me and said my faults were old,
familiar tunes that might be taught to dance.
This is fairyland, and the land of fairies.
Time will tell. But the priest and his daughter died,
as in the old story, Robert Mannying of Brunne
my first best teacher, you following close behind.

Handlyng Synne

Robert Mannyng of Brunne

What we know of the fourteenth-century poet Robert Mannyng
of Brunne derives from his own works. He was born in Brunne,
the modern Bourne, in Lincolnshire, and probably spent some time
in Cambridge. He belonged to the Gilbertine Order. Sempringham
was the headquarters of the order, and the dependent priory of Sixhill
in North Lincolnshire was nearby. He may have been a canon or
a lay brother.

His most famous work, begun in 1303, was the long poem *Handlyng
Synne*, a collection of traditional tales retold with a clear didactic
moral intention as *exampla*. With its vigorous language and humane
sympathies, the retellings of *Handlyng Synne* offer the best picture
we have before Langland and Chaucer of medieval English life.

'The Dancers of Colbek' is one of the most vivid and lively of these
retellings. As it stands in *Handlyng Synne*, it purports to be a warning
to people of what might happen to them if they dance in a church
graveyard. The original tale on which it is based, however, was
probably a pagan warning of the dangers of interfering with sacred
or magical dancers.

In Mannyng's version, the Christian priest who curses the dancers
is the one who finally suffers, both he and his daughter dying. That
casually mentioned daughter gives the game away. The dancers, who
cannot stop dancing in their ecstasy of trance, appear to be dancing
in paradise or fairyland, unable to feel either snow or hail.